CGP

# Discover & Learn

# Geography

## Years 3-4

This book is for pupils studying KS2 Geography in Years 3 and 4 (ages 7-9).

It's full of facts, sources and questions covering 'Locational Knowledge' and 'Human and Physical Geography' — perfect for exploring and understanding these topics.

**Glossary and OS® Map Key**

All the orange words in this book are explained in the glossary.
So if you don't know what an orange word means, you can look it up on pages 40-42.
This book also contains some Ordnance Survey® maps. Inside the back cover of this book there's a key that tells you what the symbols on these maps mean.

# Acknowledgements


Cover photo (Earth) © iStockphoto.com/Tolga TEZCAN.

Some paragraphs in this book are based on real-life events. However, some situations, characters and dialogue have been changed or invented for dramatic purposes – any similarity to a person, living or deceased, in these areas is merely coincidence.

This product includes mapping data licensed from Ordnance Survey® © Crown copyright 2014. Ordnance Survey Licence No. 100034841

Graphics used through this book: (blue push pin) © iStockphoto.com/blackred. (lined paper) © iStockphoto.com/subjug.

**Section One — The World**

p2 (Earth view) © iStockphoto.com/IndianSummer. p2 (beach ball) © iStockphoto.com/Taylor Hinton. p2 (world topographic map) © iStockphoto.com/xingmin07. p2-3 (night sky) © iStockphoto.com/knickohr. p3 (world map projection) The world on Mollweide projection by Strebe, Licensed under the Creative Commons Attribution-Share Alike 3.0. Unported license. http://creativecommons.org/licenses/by-sa/3.0/deed.en. p4 (man in snow) © iStockphoto.com/Ysbrand Cosijn. p4 (Madrid woman) © iStockphoto.com/Maridav. p4 (woman with coffee) © iStockphoto.com/Fotosmurf03. p5 (Arabian man) © iStockphoto.com/nullplus. p6 (world map) © iStockphoto.com/Pingebat. p6 (Britain and Ireland satellite image) Courtesy of NASA. p8 (Europe map) © iStockphoto.com/nicoolay. p11 (Mount McKinley) © iStockphoto.com/TT. p11 (Chichen Itza) © iStockphoto.com/Dario Lo Presti. p11 (Niagara Falls) © iStockphoto.com/Aivolie. p12 (Costa Rica) © iStockphoto.com/tzooka. p12 (Amazon rainforest) © iStockphoto.com/Atelopus. p13 (Aconcagua) © iStockphoto.com/MichalWloch. p13 (San Rafael Falls) © iStockphoto.com/Atelopus. p13 (Torres del Paine range) © iStockphoto.com/MogensTrolle. p13 (sand dune, Vale de la Luna) © iStockphoto.com/AnaDruga. p13 (toucan) © iStockphoto.com/deslover.

**Section Two — The UK**

p14 (Britain and Ireland satellite image) Courtesy of NASA. p15 (Pier Head, Liverpool) © iStockphoto.com/SAKhanPhotography. p15 (Evening light on the Clyde) © iStockphoto.com/NoelBennett. p15 (woman) © iStockphoto.com/Roll6. p15 (city boy) © iStockphoto.com/Blacqbook. p15 (Birmingham) © iStockphoto.com/feraru nicolae. p16 (UK topographic map) Topographic map of the United Kingdom by Captain Blood, Licensed under the Creative Commons Attribution-Share Alike 3.0. Unported license. http://creativecommons.org/licenses/by-sa/3.0/deed.en. p16 (the Quiraing, Isle of Skye) © iStockphoto.com/MaxMichelMann. p17 (Ben Nevis) © iStockphoto.com/JanBer405. p17 (Slieve Donnard) © iStockphoto.com/capri92x. p17 (Wastwater) © iStockphoto.com/krzych-34. p17 (the Pennines) © iStockphoto.com/WITTYSNAPPER. p17 (Snowdon horseshoe) © iStockphoto.com/esentunar. p18 (alpine stream) © iStockphoto.com/mtnSnail. p19 (Atcham bridge) © iStockphoto.com/Maisna. p20 (wide beach) © iStockphoto.com/zazen-photography. p20 (Rhossili Beach) © iStockphoto.com/robfordphotography. p20 (Robin Hood's Bay) © iStockphoto.com/johnbraid. p20 (Worbarrow Bay) © iStockphoto.com/kodachrome25. p20 (Durdle Door, Dorset) © iStockphoto.com/marcoregalia. p20 (Old Harry sunset) © iStockphoto.com/Gleeker. p21 (Spurn Head, Humberside) © UNIVERSITY OF CAMBRIDGE COLLECTION OF AIR PHOTOGRAPHS/SCIENCE PHOTO LIBRARY. p21 (grassy sand dunes) © iStockphoto.com/redrex. p21 (Aberdeen, Scotland) © iStockphoto.com/Peter Burnett. p21 (Brighton Beach) © iStockphoto.com/Khrizmo. p21 (Padstow harbour) © iStockphoto.com/rachel dewis. p22 (UK at night) © FELIX PHARAND-DESCHENES, GLOBAIA/SCIENCE PHOTO LIBRARY.

**Section Three — Physical Geography**

p24 (icicle) © iStockphoto.com/andhal. p24 (blue sky) © iStockphoto.com/millerpd. p26 (rushing water) © iStockphoto.com/HowardGrill. p27 (aerial river) © iStockphoto.com/Dariusz Paciorek. p27 (Rio de la Plata) © iStockphoto.com/ToniFlap. p28 (cracks on dry ground) © iStockphoto.com/Megaloman1ac_Russia. p30 (volcano eruption) © iStockphoto.com/Beboy_ltd. p30 (volcano dynamics) © iStockphoto.com/jeremkin. p31 (Soufriere Hills volcano) © iStockphoto.com/MichaelUtech. p31 (map of the Americas) © iStockphoto.com/abzee. p31 (technician in laboratory) © iStockphoto.com/omgimages. p31 (senior lady) © iStockphoto.com/diego_cervo. p31 (old man) © iStockphoto.com/Juanmonino. p32 (sound wave) © iStockphoto.com/barisonal. p32 (earthquake graph) © iStockphoto.com/Sebastien_B. p33 (Sichuan earthquake) © iStockphoto.com/pestanarui. p33 (buried house) © iStockphoto.com/stevenmayatt.

**Section Four — Human Geography**

p34 (Everest peak) © iStockphoto.com/Arsgera. p34 (cattle) © iStockphoto.com/Stolk. p34 (summer landscape) © iStockphoto.com/ISerg. p34 (Monument Valley) © iStockphoto.com/stevenallan. p34 (Piedmont hilltop) © iStockphoto.com/pjgs. p36 (Bibury) © iStockphoto.com/Antonel. p36 (English village) © iStockphoto.com/kodachrome25. p37 (Llandudno) © iStockphoto.com/ShaunWilkinson. p37 (Edinburgh at dusk) © iStockphoto.com/ShaunWilkinson. p37 (Manchester districts) Numbered districts of Greater Manchester county, by Nilfanion & Rcsprinter 123, Licensed under the Creative Commons Attribution-Share Alike 3.0. Unported license. http://creativecommons.org/licenses/by-sa/3.0/deed.en. p38 (coal industry) © iStockphoto.com/nito100. p38 (flames and embers of coal) © iStockphoto.com/tucko019. p39 (windmills) © iStockphoto.com/JoseIgnacioSoto. p39 (dam) © iStockphoto.com/jhutchin. p39 (reservoir) © iStockphoto.com/kokleong.

**Inside Back Cover**

(East bay countryside) © iStockphoto.com/ChrisMR. (old blank paper) © iStockphoto.com/tomograf. (modern compass) © iStockphoto.com/StockPhotosArt. (fingerprint) © iStockphoto.com/milosluz. (coffee cup stain) © iStockphoto.com/tarasov_vl.

# Contents




Published by CGP

Written by Rachel Murray

Editors: Charlotte Burrows, Gordon Henderson, Rachael Marshall, Sarah Pattison, Sam Pilgrim, Rachael Rogers, Sarah Williams

Reviewers: Alison Griffin, Mary-Ann Parsons, Maxine Petrie

Consultant: Rachel Clark

ISBN: 978 1 78294 211 5

With thanks to Joe Brazier and Karen Wells for the proofreading.

With thanks to Jan Greenway for the copyright research.

Printed by Elanders Ltd, Newcastle upon Tyne

Clipart from Corel®

# Section One – The World

## The Globe

The planet we live on is called Earth. It is a ball of rock spinning in space and it's absolutely huge. To walk non-stop around the middle of it would take a whole year!

*Imagine you were a giant and could pick up the Earth. What would it feel like in your hands?*

This is what the Earth looks like from outer space.

### How do you make a round thing flat?

To help us find our way around, we need a picture of where everything is — a map.

The Earth is a sphere — a ball shape.
A globe is a copy of what Earth looks like.
Some globes even have bumps for the mountains.

Globes are not a great shape to carry round though, so it's easier to have the Earth drawn flat... but how do you make a round thing flat?

*Imagine letting all the air out of a beach ball. Would you be able to lay it out flat on the ground, so you could see the whole surface? What about if you cut it open so you could spread it out more?*

Trying to make a round thing flat isn't easy. In fact, it's impossible.

Look at this picture. The Earth has been made to look flat. But the top and the bottom have been stretched, so they look bigger than they would on a globe.

## Cutting the Earth in two

To help us find our way around the world, ancient map-makers split the world up into sections. The most northern point of the Earth is the North Pole, and the most southern point is the South Pole. Imagine drawing a line around the Earth exactly half way between the two poles. This line is called the equator.

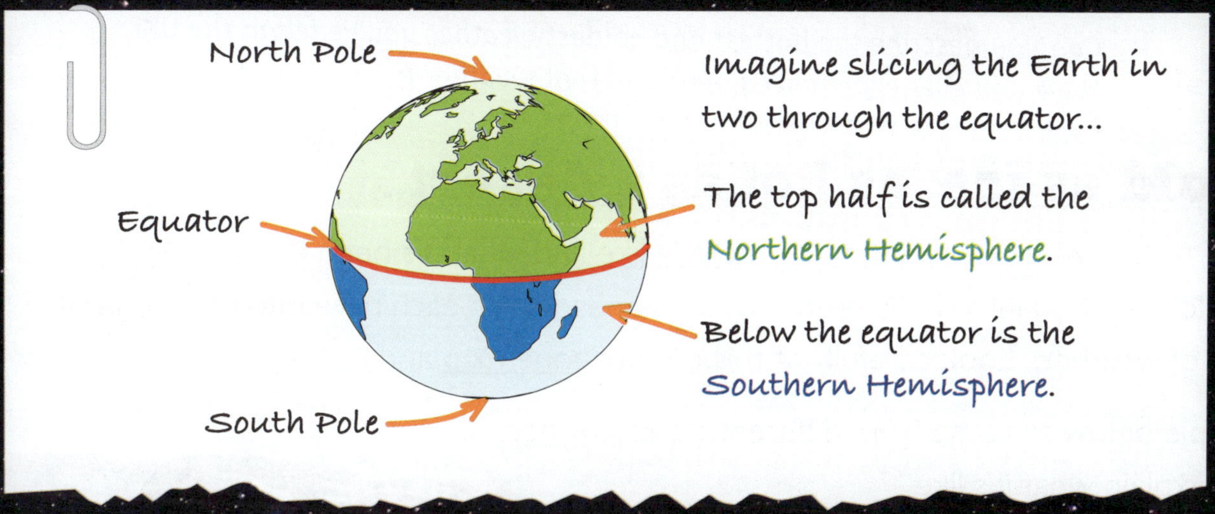


## More imaginary lines

The map makers didn't stop with the equator. They thought up lots more imaginary lines.

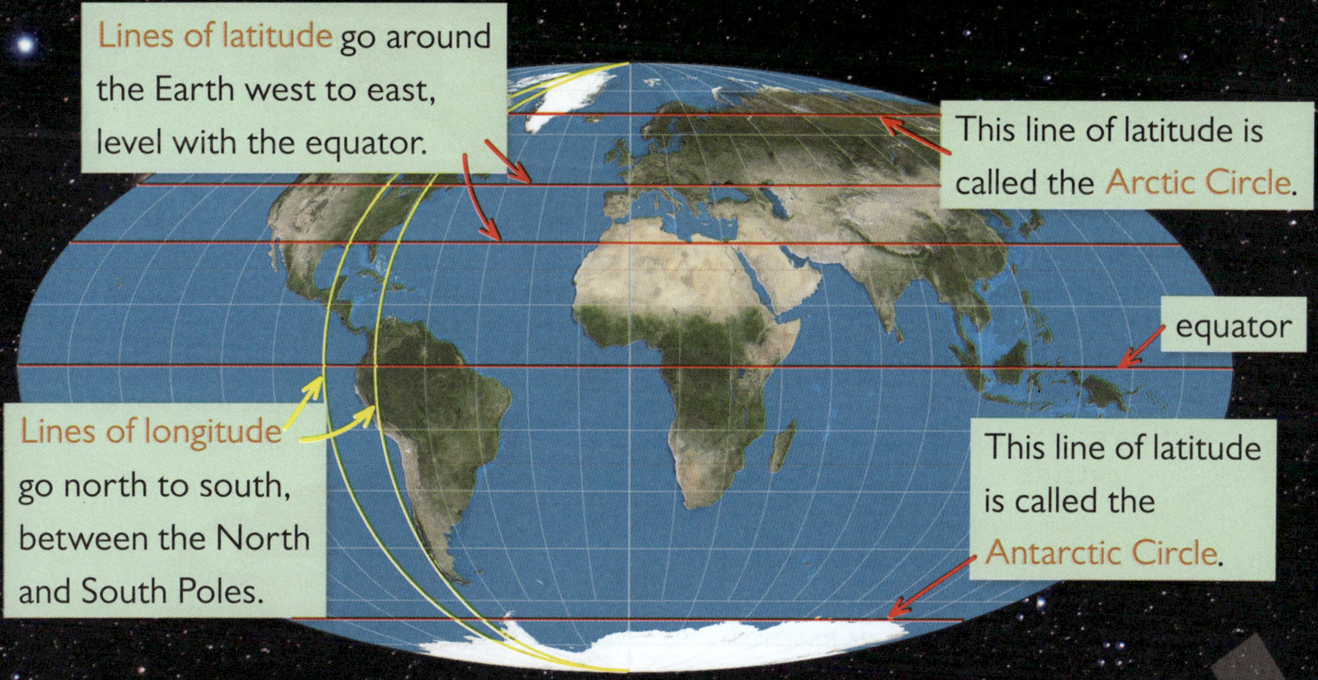


*Do you think lines of longitude are all the same length? What about lines of latitude?*

### Lots of lines going round and round...

Lines of longitude are all the same length. Lines of latitude are different lengths depending on which bit of the Earth they go round — the equator's the longest as it goes round the middle. When they're drawn on a map, the lines can have labels like 20° North or 100° West.

# Climate Zones

In the UK, the weather feels like it's always changing — sometimes it's wet, sometimes dry, sometimes sunny and sometimes it's cloudy. But, here it doesn't get as hot as Africa or as cold as the Arctic.

*Can you describe the hottest and coldest weather you've felt in the UK?*
*Have you ever experienced very different weather in another country?*

## As cold as ice, as hot as a desert...

'Climate' means what the weather is generally like and what it's been like for years. The world is split up into six different climate zones, which each have different general patterns of weather. Look carefully at this climate zone map and its key.

The people below all come from different climate zones. They all explain what it's like to live where they live.

*Which climates sound hard to live in? Why?*
*Nobody here is from a temperate climate. Can you describe one?*

## KEY

**POLAR** — Very cold and dry all year. Found in areas around the North and South Poles.

**TEMPERATE** — Cold winters and mild summers. Found in the UK.

**DESERT** — Dry all year. Some deserts are very hot all year, others have really cold winters. Also known as an 'arid' climate.

**MEDITERRANEAN** — Mild winters and dry, hot summers. Found mainly around the Mediterranean Sea.

**TROPICAL** — Hot and wet most of the year. Found around the equator where rainforests grow.

**MOUNTAINS** — Very cold all year. Found in high, mountainous areas.

'Mild' means not too hot and not too cold. Mild winters are not too cold and mild summers are not too hot.

*The climate of a place affects lots of different things. What do you think might be affected by climate? List as many things as you can.*

## Climates – hot or cold, wet or dry?

Climate affects all sorts of things. For example, the plants and animals that live in a place, the food that can be grown in an area and the clothes people wear.

# The World's Countries

The world is split up into seven continents. Continents are large masses of land and the islands that are closest to them. Each one of the world's many different countries is part of a continent.

*Look at the map of the world's continents below. What do you think separates most of the continents from each other?*

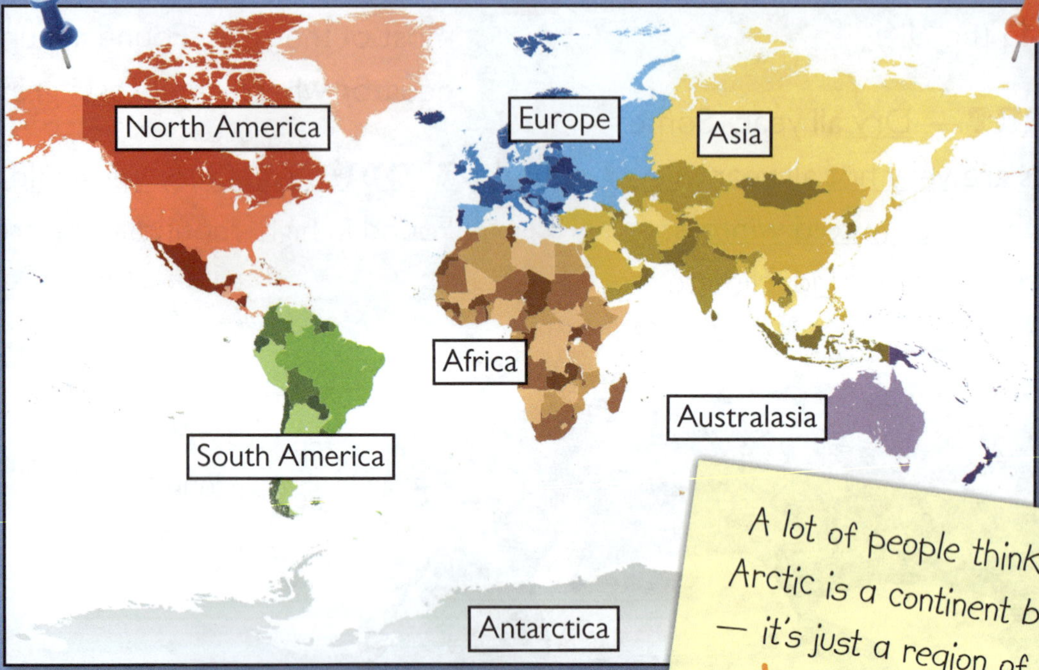


A lot of people think that the Arctic is a continent but it's not — it's just a region of ocean, ice and land.

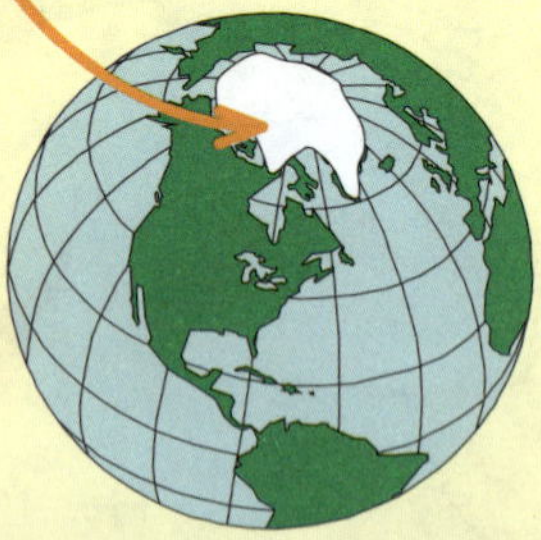

*One of the world's continents has no people living on it. Can you think which one it might be and why?*

## A small island in a big world...

The UK is part of the continent of Europe and looks like this.

Look at page 14 to see which countries make up the UK.

The UK is an island because it is surrounded by water.

*Can you find the UK on the map of the continents above?*

*Have you ever been to another island? Can you name any other islands?*

## Splitting up Europe

All of the continents have different countries in them, apart from Antarctica. That is because no one lives on Antarctica all the time. Here is a look at some of the big countries in Europe.

*Have you been to one of these countries? How was it similar to or different from the UK?*

*Compare this map to one on pages 4-5. What do you think the climate is like in Iceland? What about the climate in Greece?*

## The many countries of the world

This map shows all of the different countries in the world.

The five main oceans are labelled and so are some well-known countries.

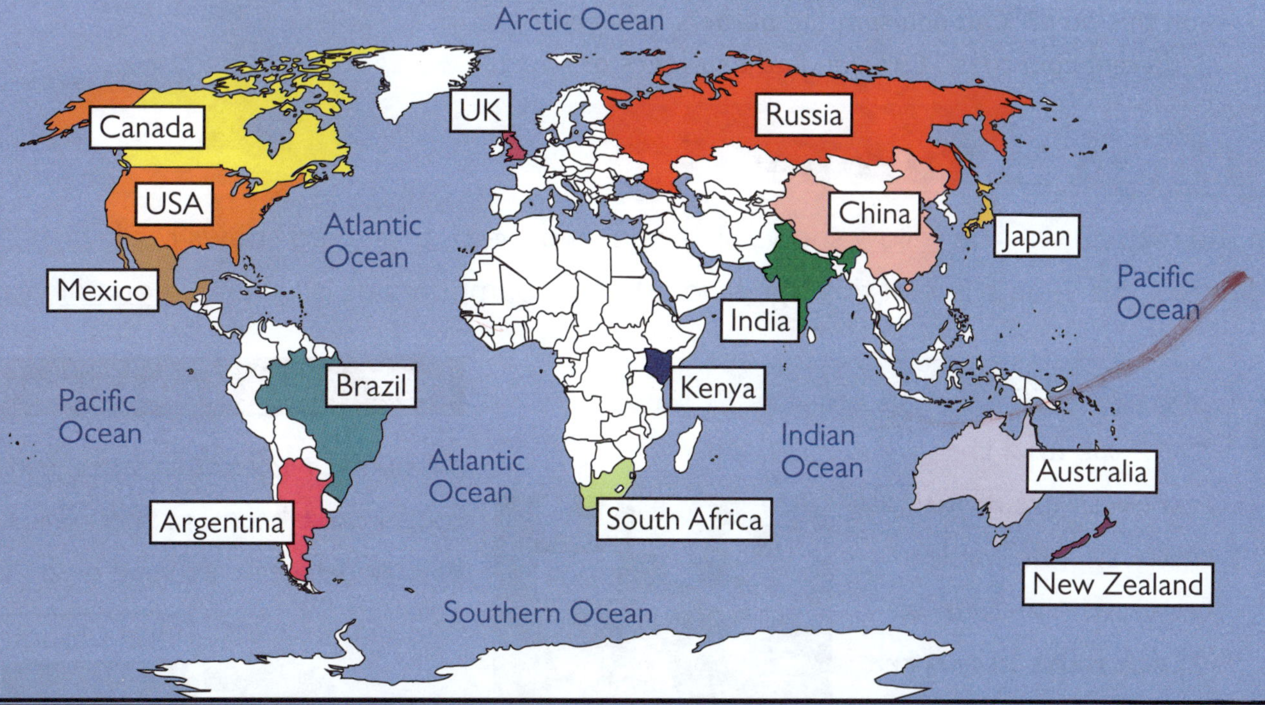


### Continents – only seven of them in our big world

The continents are separated mainly by water, which covers most of the Earth's surface. There are only seven continents but there are nearly 200 countries in the world.

# Europe and Russia

This map shows the physical geography of the continent of Europe. Physical geography means natural features, like mountains. It doesn't mean features that people have made, like roads. This map shows a few capital cities too.

This dashed line shows the edge of Europe. To the east is Asia, and to the south is Africa.

The continent of Europe and the 'European Union' or 'EU' are different. The EU is a group of countries that work together to help each other out. The continent of Europe is the land on the map above — some of its countries are in the EU and some aren't.

*What do you think orange, yellow and green mean on this map? Can you spot the borders between different countries? Can you find any lakes or rivers?*

## Up high in Europe

On the map above, the yellow shows high land, and the orangey-red shows really high land. Mountains make up some of this high land. A chain of mountains is called a mountain range.

### The Alps and the Pyrenees

The Alps and the Pyrenees are mountain ranges. The border between France and Spain runs along the Pyrenees. The Alps lie on the border of a few countries, such as Italy.

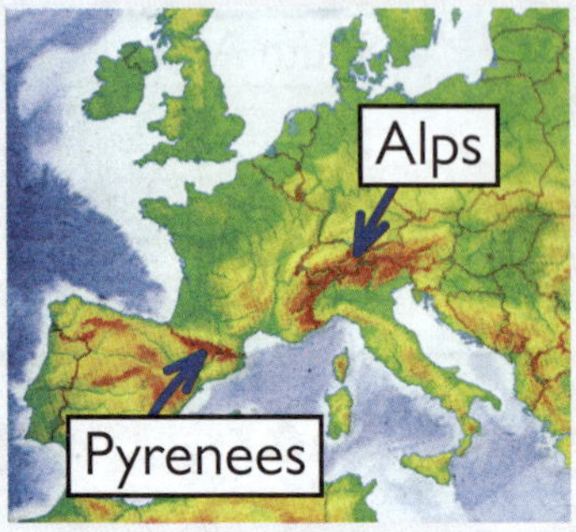


### The Ural Mountains

The Ural Mountains are really important because they form the border between Europe and Asia.

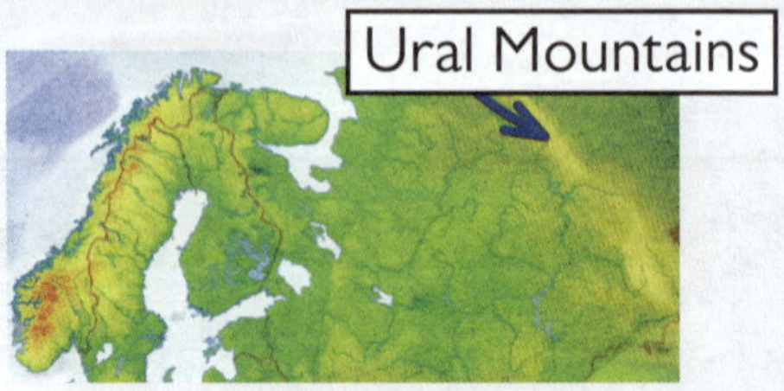

## Where water flows

This map shows the longest rivers in Europe. Rivers start on high land and flow to the sea.

*Which river do you think is the longest?*

*Can you name three rivers that end in the Black Sea?*

## The biggest of them all

Russia is the largest country in the world. It's so big you could fit more than 70 UKs into it. Part of Russia is in Europe and the rest of the country is in Asia.

*Count how many countries have a border with Russia.*

## Europe – just a small place?

### Fact Sheet: Europe

**Number of countries:** 50 (some are very small though)

**Area:** About 4,000,000 square miles (10,000,000 square km)

**Population (number of people):** About 740 million

**Largest country:** Russia (it takes up about 40% of Europe)

**Smallest country:** Vatican City (where the Pope lives)

**Longest river:** Volga in Russia

**Highest mountain:** Mount Elbrus in Russia

*Use the Internet to find out some facts about the climate in Europe.*

### Russia – one country across two continents

Most of Russia has a polar climate, so most of the country is cold and dry all year round. The rest of Europe has a mainly temperate or Mediterranean climate, so it's much warmer!

# North America

On this map of the continent of North America, the different colours show different countries.

Some of the biggest countries and cities have been labelled.

Greenland's not an independent country because it doesn't set all of its own laws (Denmark sets some).

This area of islands is called the Caribbean.

This southern part of North America is called Central America.

*How many countries on the continent can you count? Why is it difficult to count them all?*

*Where do you think would be the coldest or hottest place to live?*

## Physical geography

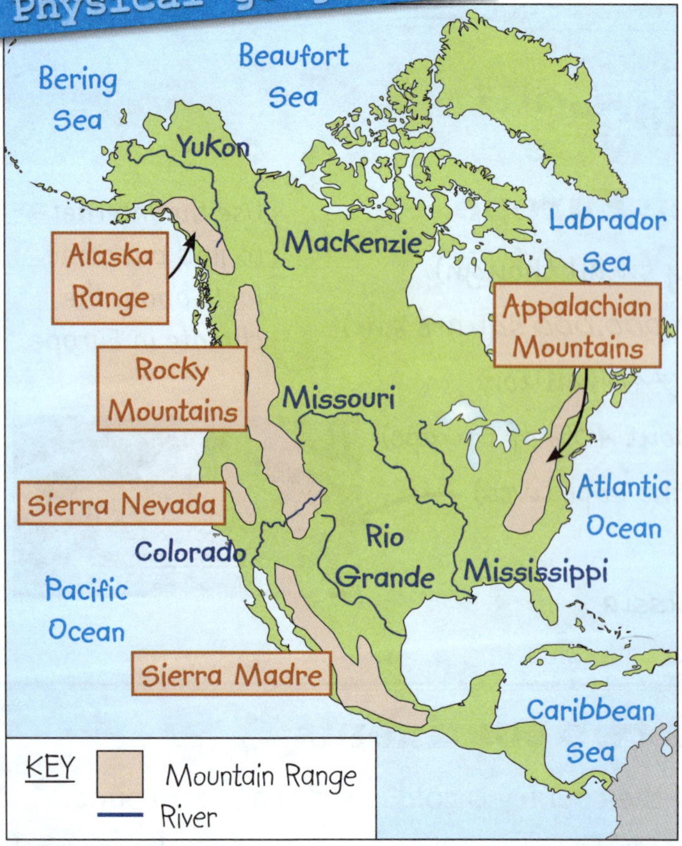


This map shows North America's physical geography — its mountain ranges, rivers and seas.

*Compare this map to the one above. Which country is the Mackenzie river in? Which country is the Sierra Madre in?*

*Point to where the Mississippi river starts. Can you follow it with your finger to where it ends?*

## More facts about North America

### Fact Sheet: North America

**Number of countries:** 24 (some countries are small islands)

**Area:** About 9,500,000 square miles (25,000,000 square km)

**Population (number of people):** About 500 million

**Largest country:** Canada

**Smallest country:** Saint Kitts and Nevis (a Caribbean island)

**Longest river:** Mississippi, USA

**Highest mountain:** Mount McKinley in the Alaska Range

Mount McKinley

Use the Internet or an atlas to find out about the lakes in North America.

## A place of adventure...

Here are some postcards from different places in North America.

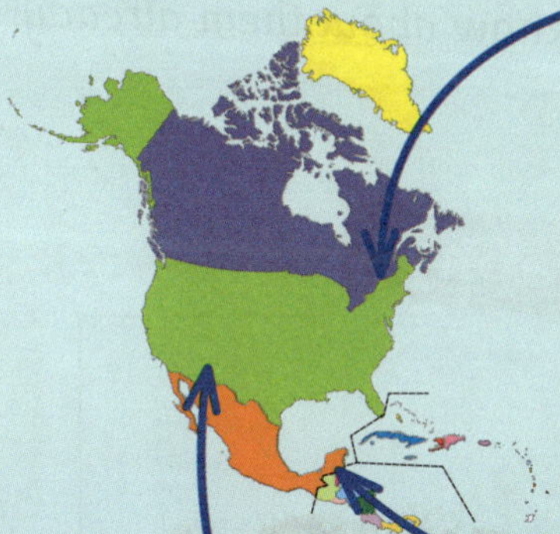

Hi! I'm visiting Niagara Falls which are huge, noisy waterfalls. One side's in Canada and the other's in the USA. We went really close to it in a boat.
Love, Erol

Wish you were here! I'm on the Yucatán Peninsula in Mexico. Tomorrow we're visiting the old ruins where the Mayan people used to live. Lots of love, Jules

Hi there! I'm visiting the Grand Canyon in the desert of southern USA. It was made by the Colorado River cutting through the rocks over millions of years.
From Yosef

### From snowy mountains to hot deserts...

North America is in many climate zones so it has some very different places. For example, Mexico has a hot tropical climate and northern Canada has a cold polar climate.

# South America

This map shows the continent of South America — the different colours show different countries. The countries have been labelled and so have some big cities.

Three places in South America actually belong to other countries. French Guiana belongs to France. The Falkland Islands and South Georgia and the South Sandwich Islands belong to the UK.

*How many different countries can you count?*

*Which (if any) of these countries have you heard of before? What do you know about them already?*

The Amazon basin is a huge area of land in South America — the photo above shows part of it. All the water in the basin will eventually drain into the Amazon river.

## The smaller America

### Fact Sheet: South America

**Number of countries:** 15
**Area:** About 7,000,000 square miles (18,000,000 square km)
**Population (number of people):** About 390 million
**Largest country:** Brazil
**Smallest country:** South Georgia and the South Sandwich Islands
**Longest river:** Amazon
**Highest mountain:** Aconcagua in the Andes in Argentina

The Aconcagua is 6959 metres high.

*Most people in South America speak Spanish or Portuguese. They're far away from Spain and Portugal, so why do you think they speak these languages?*

## Famous for lots of things

The Amazon is the largest rainforest in the world. It has an area of about 5 million square kilometres, which is mostly in Brazil. It's home to millions of different types of plants and animals. It gets smaller every day because people are chopping it down.

The Andes is the longest mountain range in the world. It covers the whole length of the west coast of South America and goes through seven different countries.

The Atacama Desert in Chile is the driest place on earth. There's only about 15 mm of rain in a whole year.

### Languages left behind...

In the past, a lot of South America was ruled by Spain and Portugal. These countries don't control any of South America today, but their languages are still used by the people there.

# Cities and Regions of the UK

The UK is short for the 'United Kingdom of Great Britain and Northern Ireland'. It's called this because four different countries are joined together, or 'united'.

The four countries in the UK are England, Wales, Scotland and Northern Ireland.

## Many parts make a whole

The UK is split up into twelve regions.

*What other areas is the UK split up into?*

Britain or Great Britain means the main island. It doesn't include the smaller islands or Northern Ireland.

The British Isles means Great Britain, the whole of the island of Ireland and all the little islands around the edges.

*Could anyone be offended if you say 'England' when you mean 'the UK'? Why?*

The Scilly Isles are part of the UK too, but they're really small so you can't always see them on maps.

# The bright lights of the city...

Each country of the UK has its own capital city where its government is based. The red dots on the map are capital cities.

What do you think the differences are between towns and cities?

Hi. I'm Heather and I'm from Glasgow. It's the biggest city in Scotland. Glasgow was famous for its shipbuilding industry along the River Clyde. People still build ships here today, but a lot of people now work in banks and other businesses too. There are lots of things to see and do — I love going to the Gallery of Modern Art and then hitting the shops!

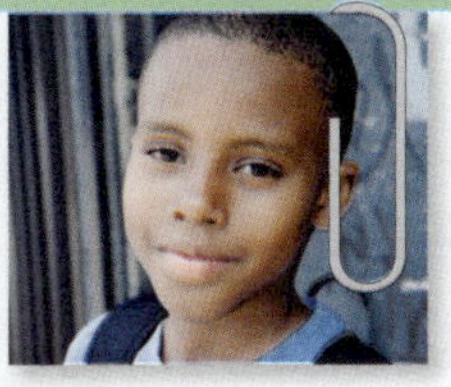

Hi. I'm Naresh and I live in Birmingham. I love it because there's an amazing mixture of people — I have friends whose families come from all over the world. You get to learn a lot about different cultures. The city is always really busy but it's beautiful. There's a mixture of old buildings and new ones. My favourite places are the cathedral and the Bullring shopping centre. The Bullring not only looks cool, but it has lots of brilliant shops and restaurants inside!

## Different cities, different people...

The people living in different regions or cities often have their own accent. Sometimes you can tell which city a person comes from by the sound of their voice!

# Mountains of the UK

Here is a map showing the main areas of high land in the UK. High land is normally made up of groups of hills or mountains. Mountains are steeper and higher than hills.

There's more about the areas labelled 1-5 on the next page.

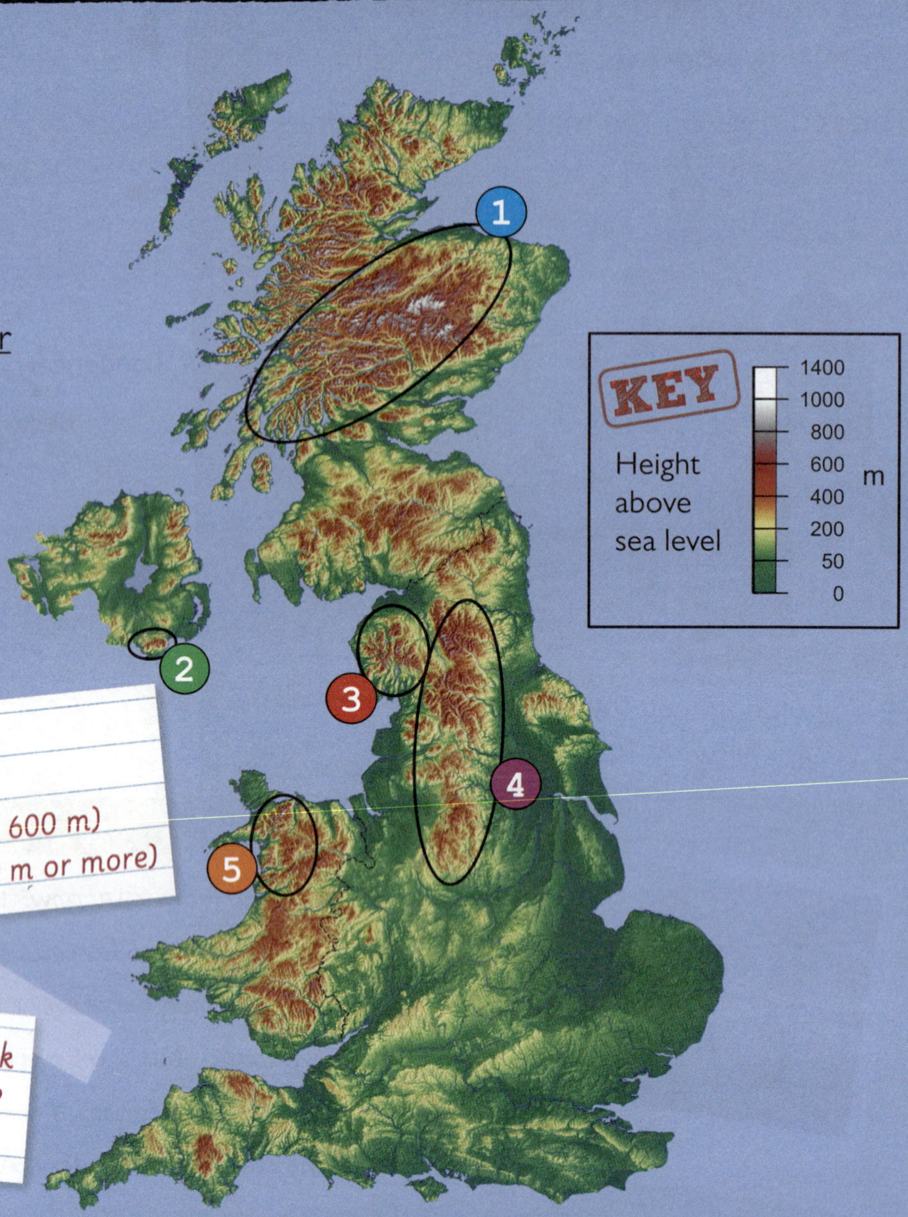


*Use the key to help you find:*
*– low land (below 400 m)*
*– areas of high land (400 m to 600 m)*
*– areas of very high land (600 m or more)*

*Which country do you think has the highest mountains? Use the key to help you.*

## How high?

Contours are lines drawn on maps that show you how high the land is above sea level. Every point on a contour line is at the same height. Some contours are numbered. The number tells you the height in metres of everything along that line.

The contours on OS® maps normally go up in 5 m or 10 m jumps. This means you can work out the height shown by any contour line.

The closer the contour lines are together, the steeper the slope.

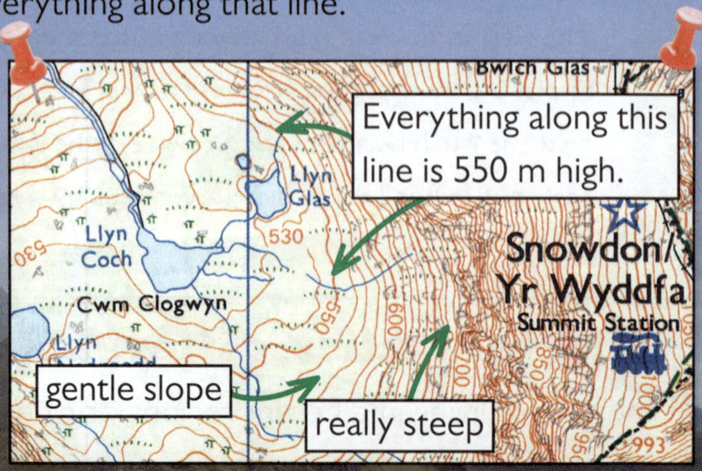

## 1. THE GRAMPIAN MOUNTAINS

These take up most of northern Scotland. They include Ben Nevis (which is the UK's highest mountain at 1344 m) and some areas for skiing.

## 2. THE MOURNE MOUNTAINS

The highest mountains in Northern Ireland. A 35 km wall crosses 15 of the summits. One of them is the highest mountain in Northern Ireland — Slieve Donard at 850 m.

## 3. THE LAKE DISTRICT

An area of lakes and mountains containing England's highest mountain, Scafell Pike at 978 m.

## 4. THE PENNINES

An area of hills and mountains that form a line through the middle of England.

*Use an atlas or the Internet to find another area of mountains in the UK.*

## 5. SNOWDONIA

An area of mountains containing the highest mountain in Wales — Snowdon at 1085 m.

### Which is the biggest of them all?

Ben Nevis is the highest mountain in Scotland and the UK. At 1344 metres high, it's about as high as 300 double-decker buses stacked on top of each other.

# Rivers of the UK

The water in most rivers starts off as rain or snow falling on high land. The water flows downhill and forms streams. These streams join together to make rivers. Rivers eventually flow into the sea.

Can you think of anything a river a might flow into before reaching the sea?

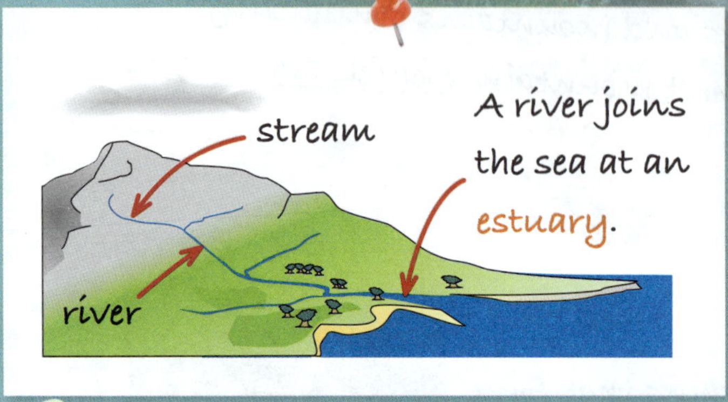

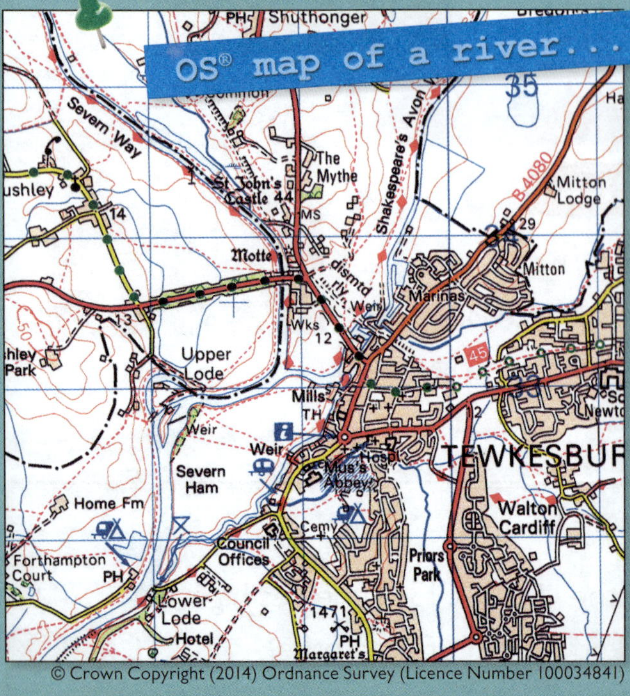




Can you spot any places on this map where two rivers join up?

Can you spot any small streams on this map?

# The River Severn

## Beautiful and useful

The River Severn is the longest river in the UK. It is 354 km (220 miles) long from its source (start point) to where it meets the sea. Its source is an area of boggy ground high up in the mountains in Wales. After Wales, it flows into England and gets wider as other rivers join it, before it flows into the sea at the Severn Estuary.

In the past, the River Severn had many different uses...

**DEFENCE**

This bend in the river helped Shrewsbury protect the English border from the Welsh.

**INDUSTRY**

At Ironbridge, the river was used to make and transport iron.

**TRANSPORT**

The river was once full of boats transporting goods such as iron, coal and clay. Stourport was a port where boats would load and unload their goods.

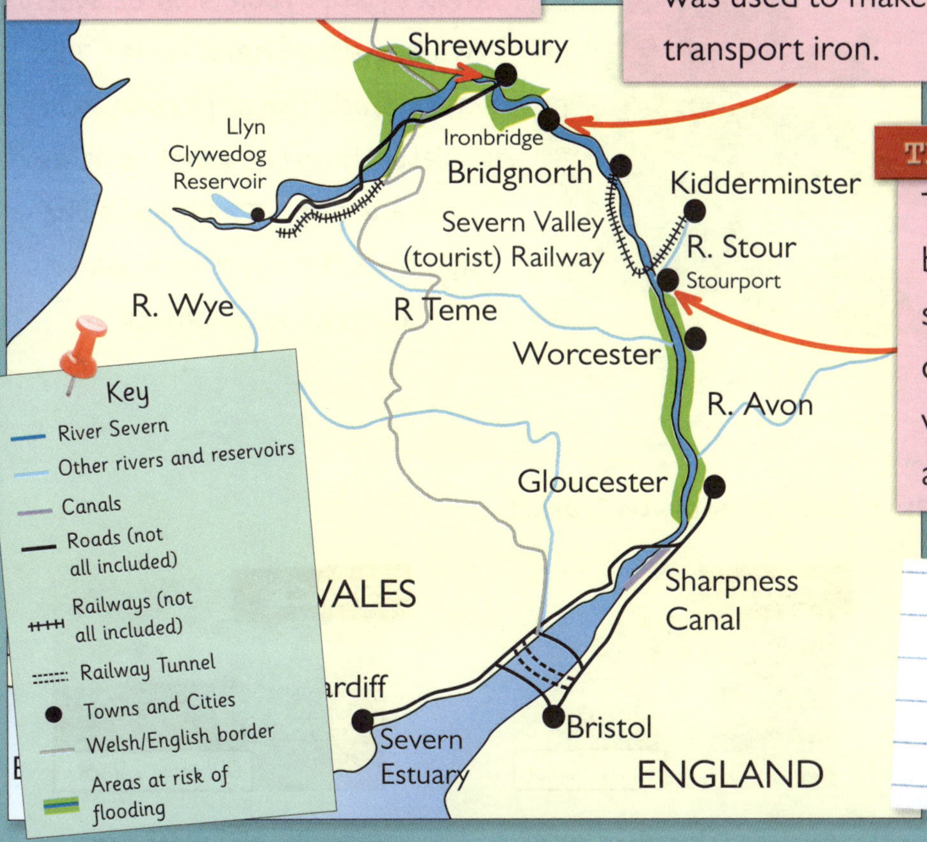


*Do you think we use the River Severn in the same ways now as we did in the past? What do you think might have changed?*

### A river runs from the mountains to the sea

The ways we use the River Severn have changed a lot. Nowadays the river isn't used very much by industry or for transport. It's used for irrigation (watering crops) and is a tourist attraction — people visit it to look at it, fish in it, take boat rides or even surf on it!

# Coastal Regions of the UK

Coastal regions are any bits of land that are next to the sea. Waves are constantly crashing onto the coast. They either erode the rock they hit, or they deposit material (e.g. mud and sand) that has been carried by the water. There are many different types of coastal landforms (features).

## BEACH

Wales

Beaches are made when material carried by sea water is deposited.

*Have you ever been to a beach? What was it like?*

## BAY AND HEADLAND

Robin Hood's Bay

Bays are formed where a band of soft rock sits between two bands of hard rock. The waves erode the soft rock more quickly than the hard rock and make a gap. The gap is the bay, and the hard rock bands become headlands.

Here are some great examples of erosion in Dorset.

## CAVE

These caves formed because water got through cracks in the rock and made these cracks bigger over time.

## ARCH

Durdle Door

Arches like this are formed when caves are eroded until the water breaks through.

## STACK

Old Harry Rocks

Eventually the top of an arch collapses, leaving stacks of hard rock like this.

## Where the wind blows...

SAND DUNE

Sand dunes are formed when wind blows the sand from the beach inland.

SPIT

A spit is a beach that has grown out into the sea. The wind causes the waves to move sand that has been deposited on the land out to sea. The sand builds up and eventually forms a narrow bit of land, such as Spurn Head in Yorkshire.

## Down by the sea...

Coastal settlements are often seaside resorts, ports or fishing villages.

Read the letters two people have written about where they live.

Aberdeen harbour

I live in Aberdeen, on the east coast of Scotland. Aberdeen is a port with many boats transporting goods to and from it.

Brighton Beach

I live in Brighton on the south coast of England. It is a seaside resort and has a really big beach. The town has lots of things for visitors like gift shops, amusements and a pier.

### A shining light in the distance...

Some parts of the coast can be dangerous to ships. Lighthouses can be used to warn ships of the rocks, but nowadays ships also have other tools to help them find their way.

# Land Use in the UK

Land use basically means what people use land for. The map below shows a picture of the UK at night. The bright areas are caused by lights in urban areas (towns and cities). The dark areas are rural areas of the UK, such as farms, forests and wild areas.

There are a few places in the UK where it's too rocky, steep or boggy to build or grow anything. These places might still be used by walkers and bird watchers though.

*Why might there be fewer urban areas in the middle of Scotland and Wales? Think about what the land is like in these areas.*

Forestry means caring for trees. Many trees are grown to be eventually cut down and used as wood. More trees are then planted to replace them. People can enjoy walking in the forests too.

Industry means turning basic materials into products in factories, e.g. making cars. Industry is usually found in the outer parts of towns and cities.

Land outside of towns and cities is mainly used for farming.

Urban areas are filled with roads and buildings. There are often lots of offices, shops and other businesses. There are also lots of houses for people to live in, along with leisure facilities and other services (e.g. dentists).

*Why do you think most shops and businesses are in urban areas and not in the countryside?*

# The buzz of the city

These OS® maps show parts of Manchester, which is an urban area — there are lots of roads, houses, businesses and industry. The OS map below shows a large number of houses. Many people live here, so there are a lot of services (e.g. schools) in this area for them to use.

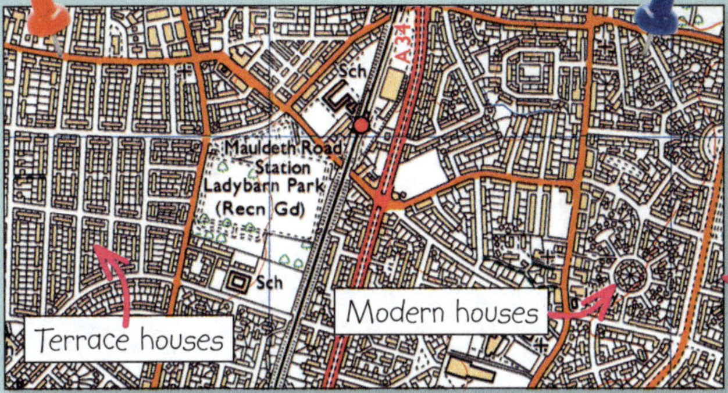


The straight rows of houses are terrace houses that were built in Victorian times for workers. Modern houses are often a bit more spaced out on curved roads and estates.

*How many schools can you see on this map?*

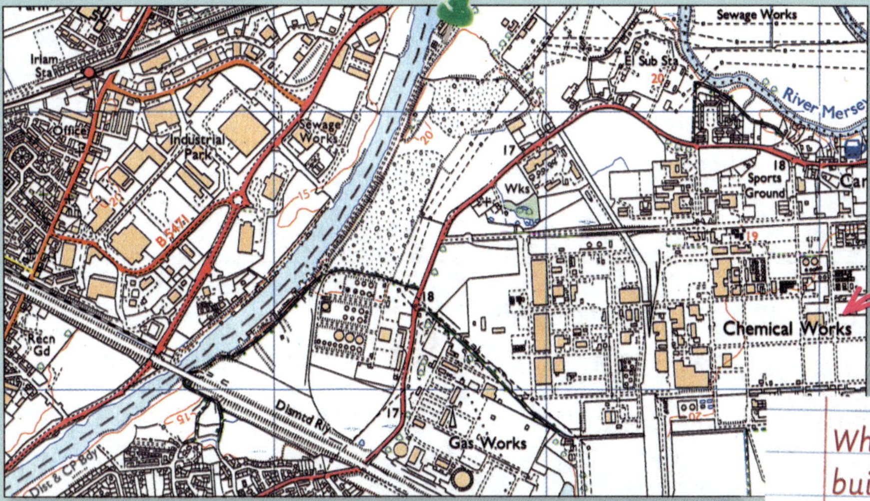


In the past, boats and trains were used to transport items to factories that they needed, e.g. coal for fuel. They also carried away what the factories made. This meant a lot of industry was built near canals and railways.

*Why do you think most new industry is built near main roads instead of canals?*

# The heart of the countryside

This OS map shows a rural area in Cumbria. In rural areas, there are fewer roads, houses and businesses, but more farmland, forestry and wild areas.

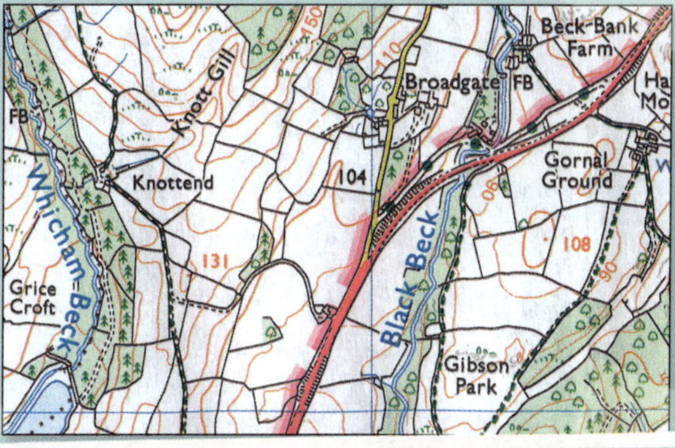


Different areas have different kinds of farm.

Flat areas are good for growing crops or rearing cattle.

In hilly areas people farm sheep.

*Look at this map. What sort of farming do you think happens here? (Have a look at page 16 to remind yourself what contours on a map show.)*

## Is there any wasted space?

Most of the land in the UK is used for something. Even land that looks like it's doing nothing is probably being used for growing crops or grazing animals.

# The Water Cycle

The pictures below all have something very important in common.

*How are the things shown in these pictures similar and how are they different?*

*Think about the water in each of the pictures above. Has it always been where it is now or was it once somewhere else? How far back can you trace its past?*

## The water cycle goes round and round

The amount of water on Earth and in the atmosphere roughly stays the same. The water just moves from place to place and changes state. Sometimes it's water vapour, sometimes it's ice or snow, and sometimes it's plain old water.

*Where does the water that we drink come from? How does it get back into the water cycle?*

START HERE

1 When water warms up, it evaporates (turns into water vapour) and rises into the air.

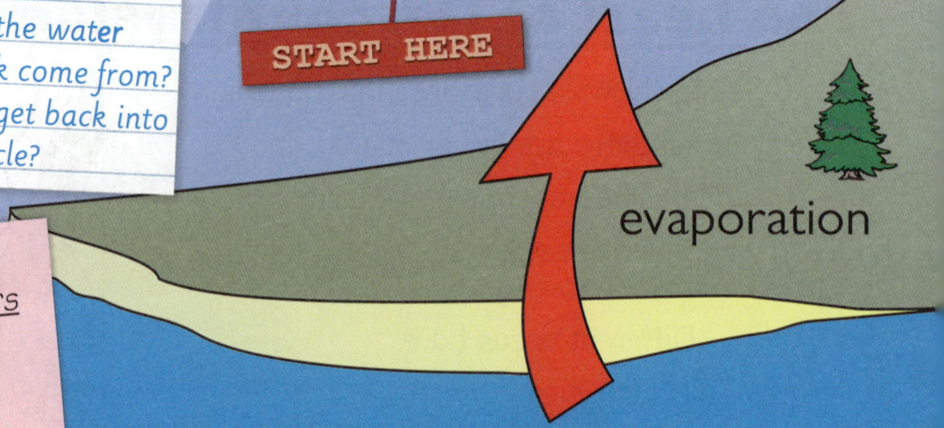


Fun Fact: Nearly three-quarters of the Earth's surface is covered in water.

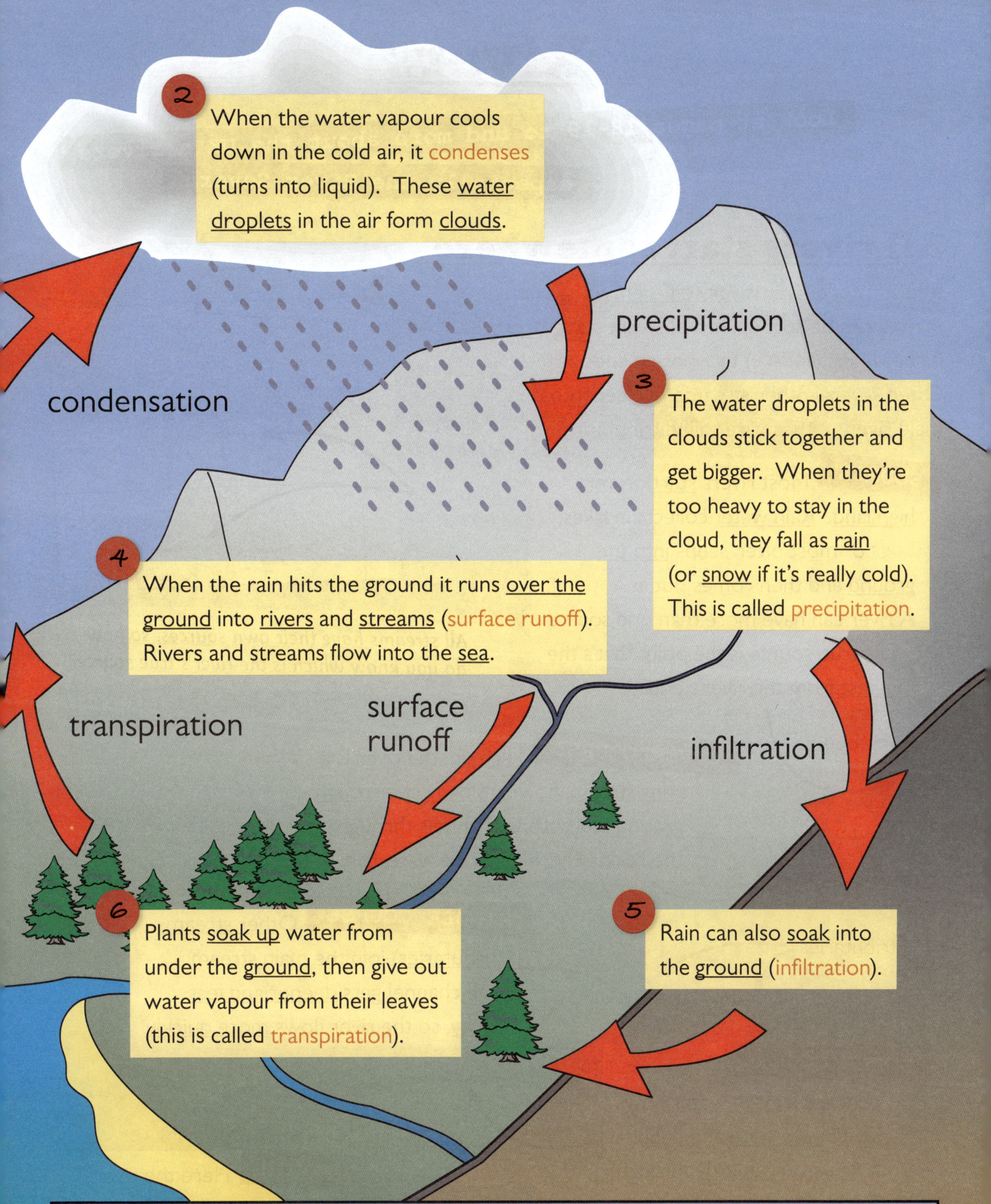


**Animals – they're part of the water cycle too...**

Animals drink water, then give it out in their urine (wee). It will then run into rivers and end up in the sea. Then the water can go through the water cycle all over again.

# Rivers

Look at pages 18-19 to find more about the UK's rivers especially the River Severn

## All rivers start somewhere

The start of a river is <u>very different</u> to its end. A river can be split up into different <u>stages</u> from its beginning (source) to where it ends at the sea. Often several other streams will feed into one main river — these are called <u>tributaries</u>.

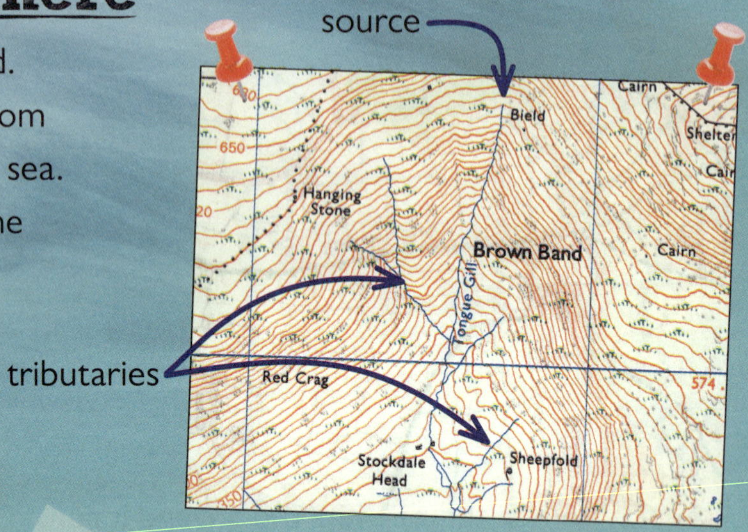


**SOURCE** Most rivers <u>start</u> on <u>very high land</u>. <u>Rain water</u> collects in lakes, bogs or most often seeps <u>into the ground</u> and then comes out as a spring. A river can have more than one source — its true source is the point that's the <u>furthest</u> from the river's end.

*All streams have their own sources, so how do you know which is the river's true source?*

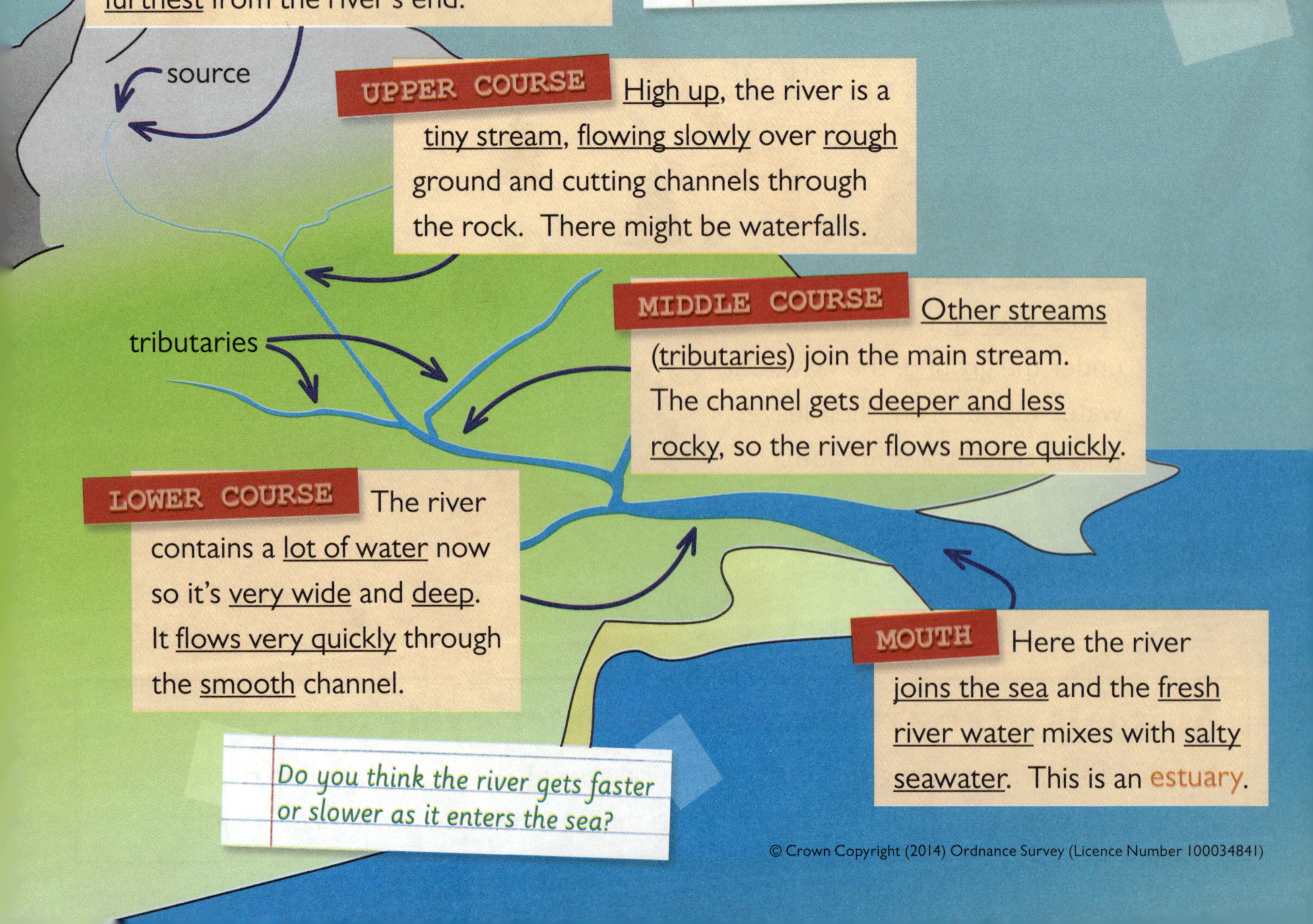


**UPPER COURSE** <u>High up</u>, the river is a <u>tiny stream</u>, <u>flowing slowly</u> over <u>rough</u> ground and cutting channels through the rock. There might be waterfalls.

**MIDDLE COURSE** <u>Other streams</u> (<u>tributaries</u>) join the main stream. The channel gets <u>deeper and less rocky</u>, so the river flows <u>more quickly</u>.

**LOWER COURSE** The river contains a <u>lot of water</u> now so it's <u>very wide</u> and <u>deep</u>. It <u>flows very quickly</u> through the <u>smooth</u> channel.

**MOUTH** Here the river <u>joins the sea</u> and the <u>fresh river water</u> mixes with <u>salty seawater</u>. This is an estuary.

*Do you think the river gets faster or slower as it enters the sea?*

## Rivers are always changing

Erosion and deposition change how rivers look.

Erosion means 'breaking down and carrying away'. A river wears down the rock where it flows. It also picks up stones and other bits (its load) that help do more erosion.

Deposition means 'dropping off'. When a river is slowed down, it doesn't have the energy to carry its load any more, so it drops it.

## Rivers like to wiggle

As water flows round a corner, it goes fastest on the outside of the bend, so the bank is worn away and forms a river cliff. On the inside it is slowed down, so it drops its load — this dropped load is called sediment.

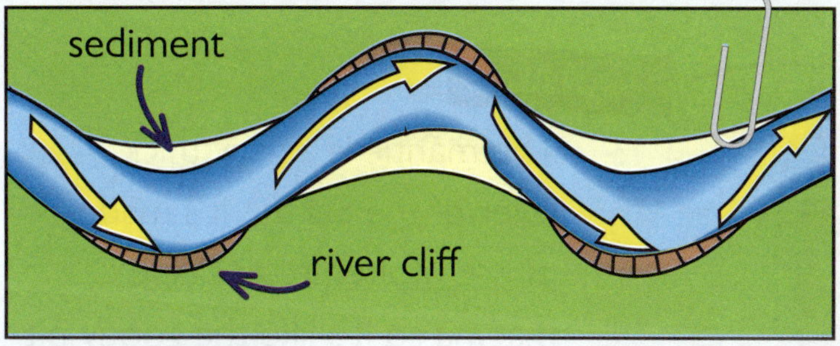

What do you think this river looked like 2000 years ago? What might it look like in another 2000 years?

Over hundreds of years, the river looks more and more wiggly — the wiggles are called meanders. They form in the middle course of a river.

## Making new land

When the lower course of a river reaches the sea, it is forced to slow down so it deposits a lot of its load as sediment. The sediment splits the channel, forming a delta. Over hundreds of years, the sediment becomes land.

### Have a go at making your own river channels...

If you flow water over some sand in a water tray, you can watch it form channels in the sand. You can control where the channels form by building up piles of sand.

# The Earth's Structure

The Earth seems nice and solid under our feet, but actually it's constantly moving about and parts of the centre of the Earth are even liquid.

## The Earth is like a Creme Egg®

If you could cut the Earth in half, you'd see that it looks a bit like a Creme Egg® — nice and solid on the outside with a gooey liquid bit inside.

The inside of the Earth is split up into different layers. Here they are:

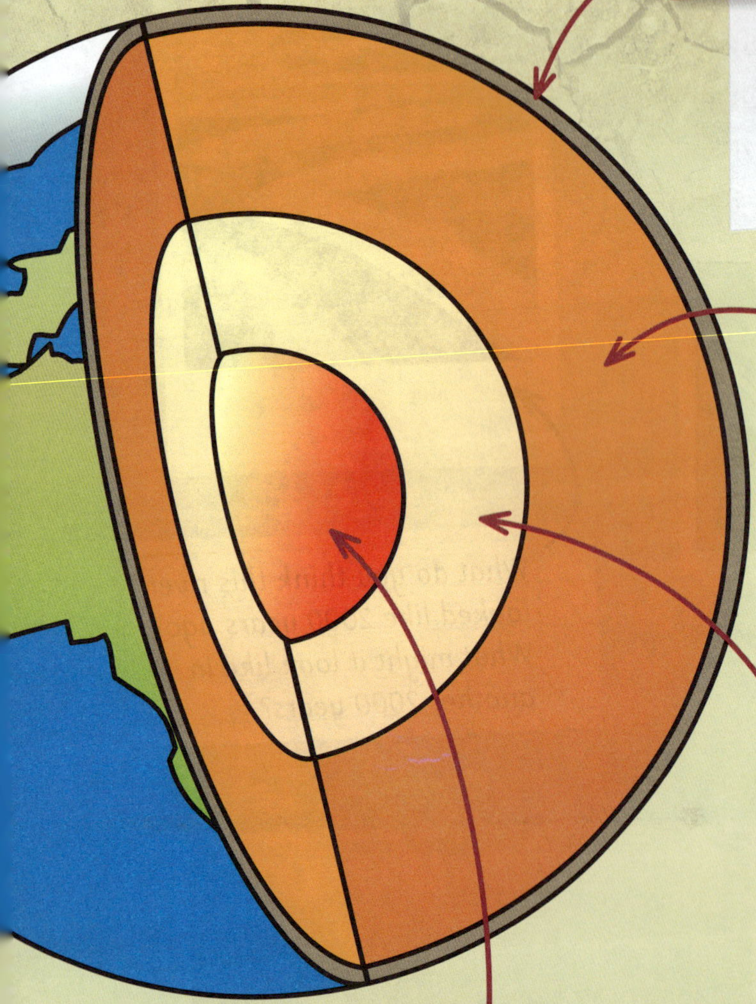

**CRUST**

The crust is the outer layer of the Earth. We live on its surface and parts of it are covered by oceans. It's really hard and solid, but is very thin compared to the other layers.

**MANTLE**

The mantle is a very thick layer of the Earth. It's made of hot molten rock called magma so it's like the gooey bit of a Creme Egg®, but really hot.

**OUTER CORE**

It gets even hotter as you get closer to the centre of the Earth. It's so hot that the outer core is a layer of proper liquid, which scientists think is made of the metals iron and nickel.

**INNER CORE**

The inner core is the centre of the Earth. It's the hottest part at about 6,000 °C, but there's so much pressure that it's solid not liquid. It's a big, super-hot, solid ball of iron and nickel.

*Can you think of any natural way that magma might be able to get to the surface of the Earth?*

## Bits of crust float and move...

The thin crust that we live on is split up into pieces called tectonic plates which 'float' on the mantle. Waves of heat come from the hot mantle and make the plates move about a little.

THE EARTH'S TECTONIC PLATES

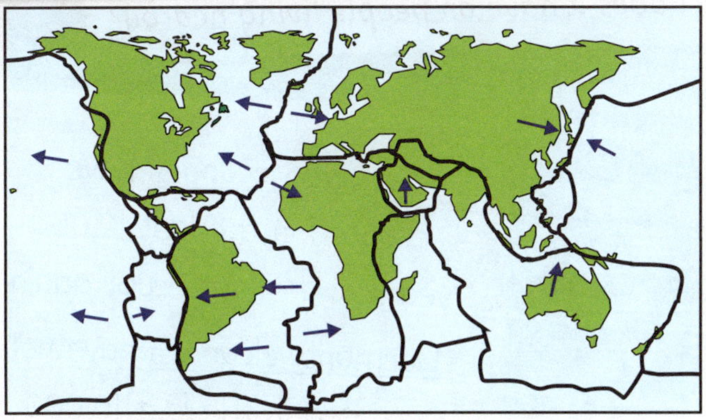

*Can you find on the map the tectonic plate that you live on? Can you feel it moving right now?*

KEY

Direction of plate movement

Tectonic Plate Boundaries

## ...which causes volcanoes and earthquakes

Volcanoes and earthquakes often happen where two plates meet.

WHERE VOLCANOES AND EARTHQUAKES HAPPEN

*Does every plate boundary have volcanoes and earthquakes?*

KEY

Volcanoes

Earthquakes

Tectonic Plate Boundaries

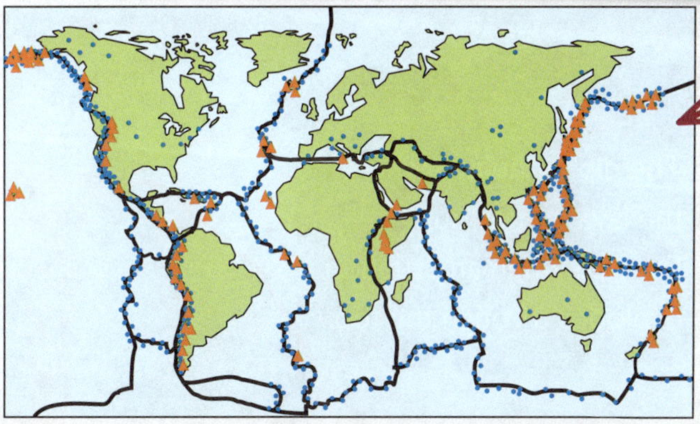

Plates move in different directions. They can move towards each other, away from each other, or just slide side by side. These movements cause earthquakes and volcanic eruptions (see the next few pages).

### Making a mountain out of a plate...

Plates don't just cause earthquakes and volcanoes. Where two plates push towards each other, mountains can build up — like the Himalayas.

# Volcanoes

*Have you ever seen a volcano?*
*What causes a volcanic eruption?*
*What effect does it have on people living nearby?*

Volcanoes are points on the Earth's crust where magma rises from the Earth's mantle to the surface and leaks (or explodes) out.

*What is the difference between magma and lava?*

When magma reaches the Earth's surface, it is called lava.

Active volcanoes have erupted in the last 10,000 years and might erupt again.
Dormant volcanoes have not erupted in the last 10,000 years, but still could.
Extinct volcanoes are ones nobody think will erupt again!

## Taking a closer look at volcanoes (but not too close!)

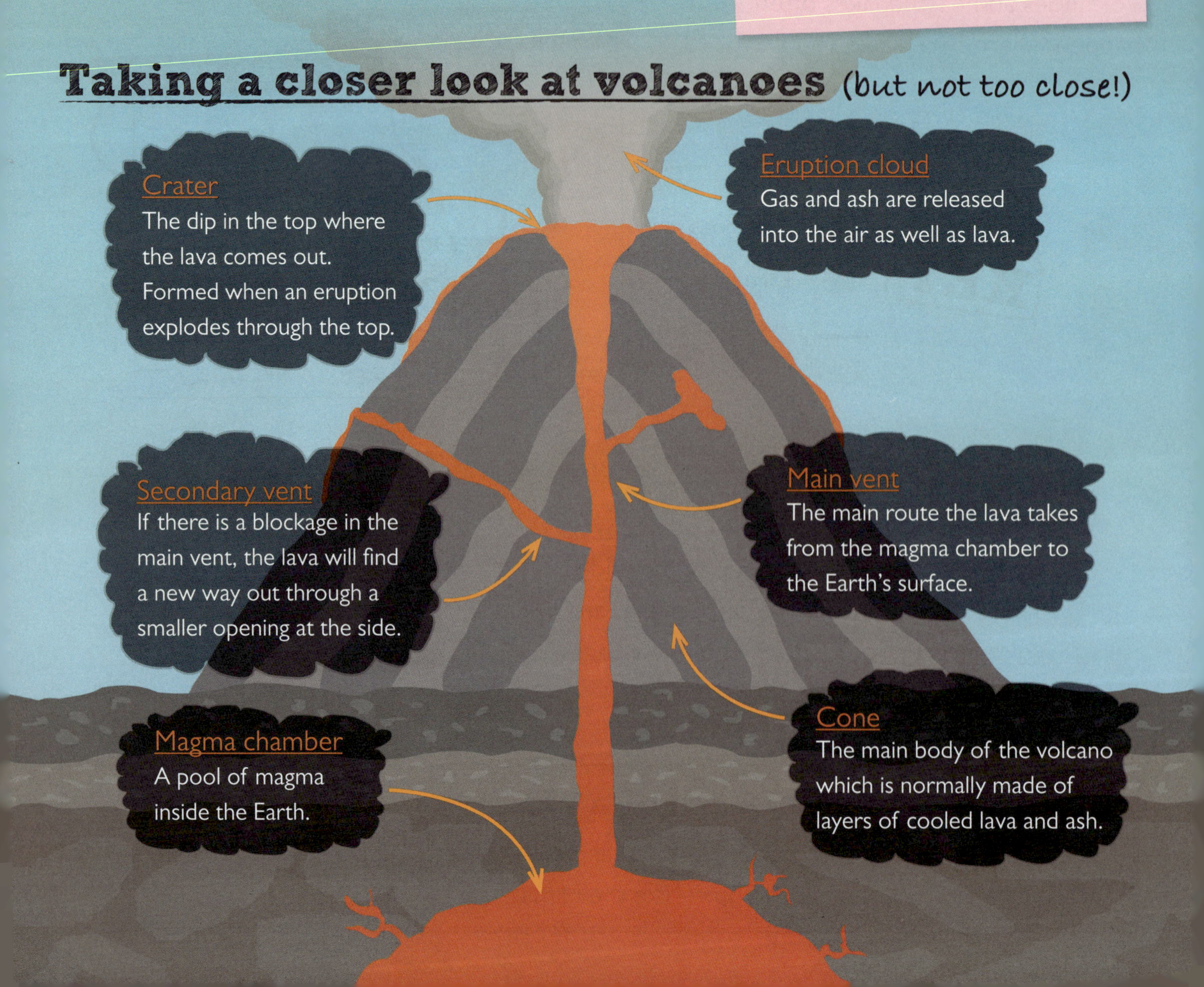

# Montserrat

## Destruction in the Caribbean

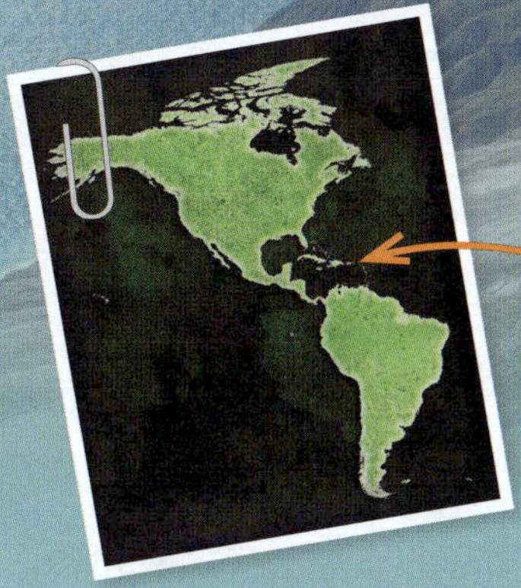

Montserrat is a beautiful Caribbean island with a volcano. The volcano was thought to be dormant, but it erupted a few times in 1997, destroying the capital city and forcing more than half of the island's people to leave their homes.

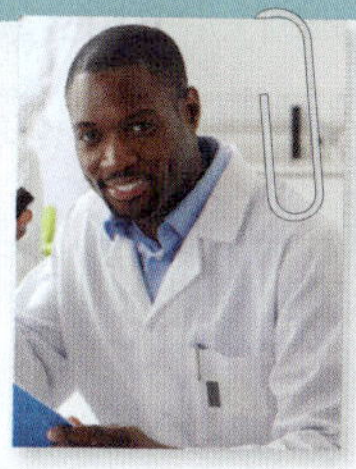

I am one of the scientists who studied the volcano before it erupted. In 1995 it started to steam and smoke, then we noticed that it was starting to change shape. We warned everyone that an eruption would happen and worked out which bits of the island were not safe. It was lucky that only 19 people were killed out of the thousands who lived here.

I used to own a gift shop in the capital city, Plymouth. It was really popular with tourists. I had to abandon it when we knew the volcano was going to erupt, and it's a good job I did as it is now buried under mud and ash. I moved to the north of the island to stay with some relatives where it is safe, but life was hard as I had no job and so much had been destroyed — even the only hospital.

I was a farmer here in Montserrat. We were offered the chance to move to the UK before the eruption but I chose to stay and look after my crops. I wish I hadn't now, as metres of lava and ash covered everything. I have no land left that I can farm, my house burned down and a few of my friends who also stayed were killed.

## Volcanoes – dangerous and deadly

You can see from the pictures here that volcanoes are dramatic when they explode. But they are also dangerous — they can damage people's houses and even kill people.

# Earthquakes

Earthquakes are when the ground starts shaking. They may only last for less than a minute, but can cause lots of damage and kill people.

*Have you ever experienced an earthquake?*
*What did it feel like and was anything damaged?*

## How do earthquakes happen?

Look back at page 29 to read up on tectonic plates which cause earthquakes.

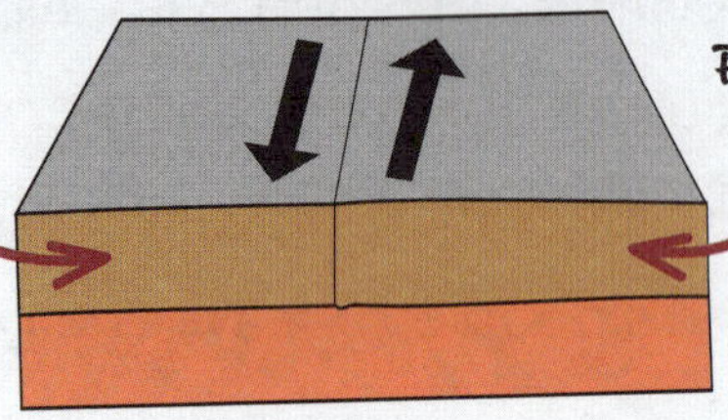


Tectonic plates are constantly moving — often forcing themselves past each other, and sometimes getting stuck.
When they get stuck, pressure builds up. Eventually, something will have to give way. When it does, the pressure is released in waves of energy which feel like shaking.

The place on the ground that is directly above where the earthquake starts is called the epicentre.

You feel an earthquake less the further away you are from the epicentre.

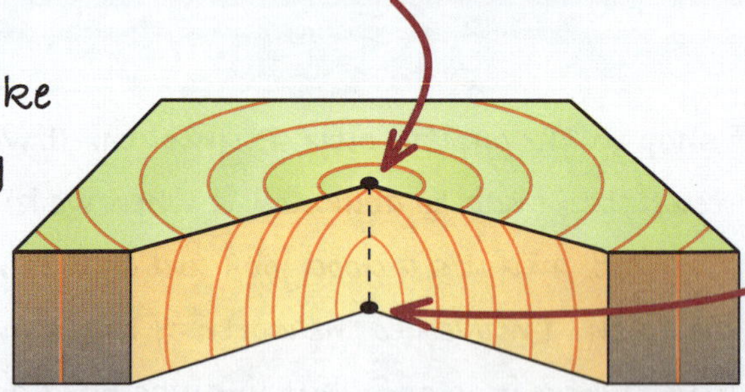

The exact place underground where an earthquake happens is called the focus.

There will often be smaller earthquakes after the first one, called aftershocks.

## Shake, rattle and roll

A machine called a seismometer can record the Earth's shaking. The strength of the shaking is measured on the Richter scale.
On the Richter scale, each number means ten times the number before it, so an earthquake measuring 4 is ten times worse than one measuring 3.

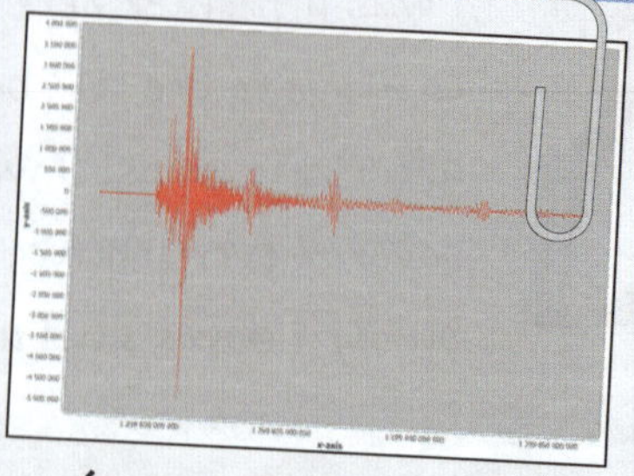

Seismometer recording

## Shaking and breaking

It's not the shaking that kills people, it's what the shaking causes...

**COLLAPSED BUILDINGS**

Buildings can trap and kill people as they fall down during an earthquake. Many people will be left homeless.

**ROADS DESTROYED**

Earthquakes cause roads and bridges to collapse, which means that the emergency services can't get through to help rescue trapped and injured people.

**LANDSLIDES**

Mud and rocks can be loosened from the sides of hills. They then flow downwards and bury houses and people. This is called a landslide.

**DISEASE**

Earthquakes can destroy power lines and water supplies, so people have no clean, safe water to drink. Under these conditions, diseases spread very quickly.

**TSUNAMIS**

If an earthquake happens at sea, giant waves called tsunamis are formed. When these waves hit land, they cause massive flooding and destroy everything for miles.

## Staying alive

Earthquakes can't be predicted accurately. In countries that get many earthquakes, lives can be saved by spending lots of money on strong, earthquake-proof buildings, roads and bridges. Following earthquake action plans can also save lives.

*What happens if countries can't afford to make buildings etc. stronger?*

Earthquake action plan:

- Have canned food, bottled water, dust masks and torches ready.
- Take cover under a table away from windows and things that might fall.
- If you are outside, stay away from trees, buildings and power lines.

### Earthquakes are happening all the time

Over a million earthquakes happen every year all over the world, but many are so small that we just don't notice them. Even the UK has about 200 earthquakes every year.

# Settlements

Settlements are where people chose to settle — to build homes and to live. Hundreds of years ago, people would have looked at the landscape to decide where to build their homes.

*Look at these different landscapes. Where do you think would be a good place to build a home? Think about what people need to survive.*

Settlements were often built on top of hills to make them harder to attack.

Wherever we live, we always need clean water to drink and food to eat to survive. We find it hard to survive in very hot and very cold places. Living close to trees means there will be lots of wood, which can be used for fires (to cook with and keep you warm) and building shelters.

# It's all in the name

Often the name of a place gives a clue to why a settlement was built there.

*Look at this map. Can you see any place names that are similar?*

Place names in Britain often share the same prefixes or suffixes. A prefix is a beginning of a word. A suffix is an ending of a word.

SCOTLAND

| | |
|---|---|
| Dun- | fort |
| Glen- | valley |
| Inver- | river mouth |

ENGLAND

| | |
|---|---|
| -ton | village |
| -ham | homestead or village |
| -ford | river crossing |
| -by | farmstead or village |
| -caster | Roman city or fort |
| -hurst | wooded hill |
| -ing | 'the people of' |
| -bury | fort |
| -ley | clearing in a wood |

NORTHERN IRELAND

| | |
|---|---|
| Bel- | river mouth |
| -magh | plain |
| -mullin | mill |

WALES

| | |
|---|---|
| Aber- | river mouth |
| Caer- | city or fort |
| Llan- | church |
| Cwm- | valley |

*Can you think of any other place names which have one of these prefixes or suffixes?*

## I'm from a wooded hill, how about you?

Most places have changed a lot since people first settled there. That means place names don't normally tell you what a place is like now, but what they used to be like.

# Types of Settlement

Most settlements started off as small places when the first people decided to live there. Some of them became really popular though and went on to grow into towns and cities.

## Hamlets are tiny

Look at the descriptions of settlements on these pages. What type of settlement do you think you live in?

THE HAMLET OF FIDDINGTON

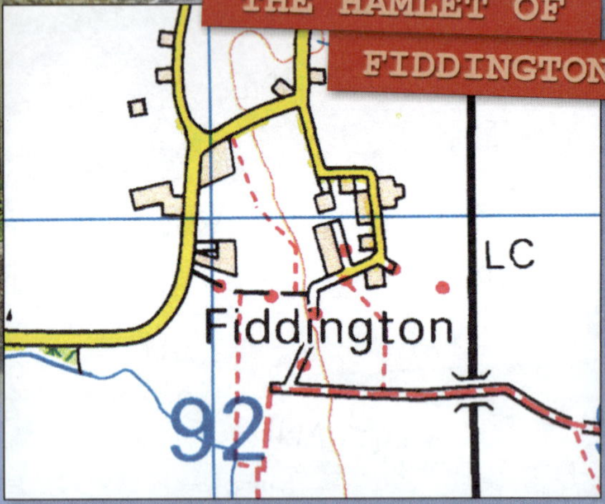


Hamlets have:

- no church
- only a few houses
- normally no shops or other businesses
- sometimes only one road
- lots of fields

## Villages – bigger than hamlets

THE VILLAGE OF CASTLE COMBE

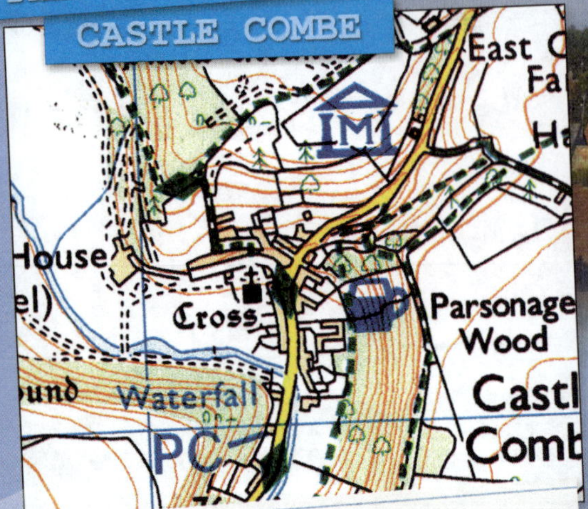

Look at the map above. Can you spot a tourist attraction? Use the key on the inside of the back cover to help you.

Villages may have:

- a church, marketplace or village green
- more houses than a hamlet
- some shops and services (like surgeries)
- some tourist attractions
- a few roads
- lots of fields

# Towns – bigger than villages

Towns have:

- local government buildings
- lots of houses
- lots of shops, offices and leisure facilities (like swimming pools)
- schools, parks and useful services
- lots of roads including some main roads

Some towns also have tourist attractions.

THE TOWN OF LLANDUDNO

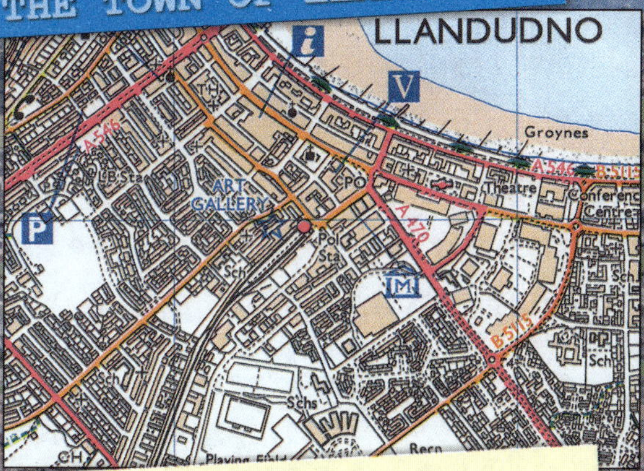


*Think about a town you know.*
*What useful services for people are there?*
*What leisure facilities are there?*

In a town (or village) there might also be some industry. For example, there might be a factory, a brewery or a chemical plant.

# Cities – bigger, brighter and busier than all

THE CITY OF EDINBURGH

A place can only be called a city when it has a charter from the Queen. Cities have the same things as towns but loads more of them. They also have:

- Local government centres
- a cathedral (but not always)
- very big roads (maybe even motorways)

Conurbations are huge urban areas — just buildings for miles and miles. They are formed when cities spread and join together, also taking over towns.

For example, Greater Manchester is made up of the City of Manchester, Salford (1), Bolton (2), Stockport (3), Oldham (4), Rochdale (5), Bury (6), Trafford (7), Tameside (8) and Wigan (9) all joined together.

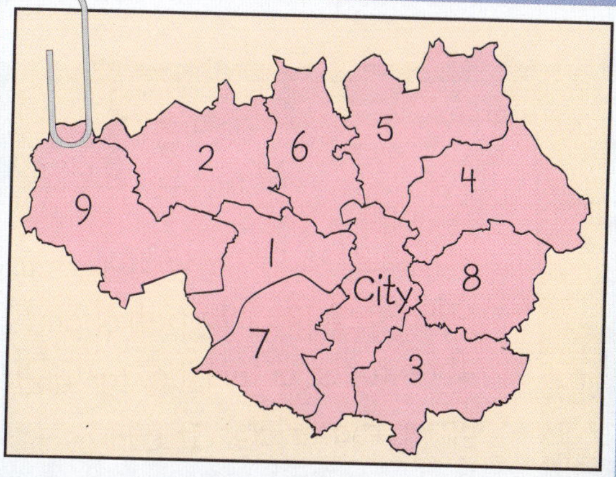


## Towns and cities can swallow each other up...

As more people want to live near a town or city, more houses, roads and facilities need to be built. This causes the town or city to grow and join up with surrounding towns.

# Natural Resources

Natural resources are all the things found in nature that we find useful. Some of these are non-renewable, which means that once we've used them up, there'll be no more. Some are renewable, so there'll be more in the future.

Coal, oil and gas are called "fossil fuels" because they come from fossilised plants and animals. They are all non-renewable resources.

## Getting power from the ground

Coal is found under the ground and can be brought to the surface by mining. It is useful to us because it can be burnt in power stations to make electricity. We used to mine loads of coal in the UK, but these days it's cheaper to buy it from other countries. This means most of our coal mines have closed.

COAL

OIL AND GAS

Crude oil and natural gas can be found underneath the sea bed. The UK gets a lot of its supply from under the North Sea. Huge platforms are built out at sea, where drills make holes in the sea bed to pump out the oil and gas.

Our supplies of coal, oil and gas are RUNNING OUT!

Crude oil is really useful — it can be made into petrol and other fuels, or plastic, tar and other materials. It can even be burnt to make electricity.

Natural gas is used for heating, cooking and to make electricity.

What do you think would happen if we did run out of oil and gas?
What do you think we could do to prepare?

## Renewable sources just keep on giving

The main renewable energy sources we use to generate electricity in the UK are wind, hydro-electric power and biomass.

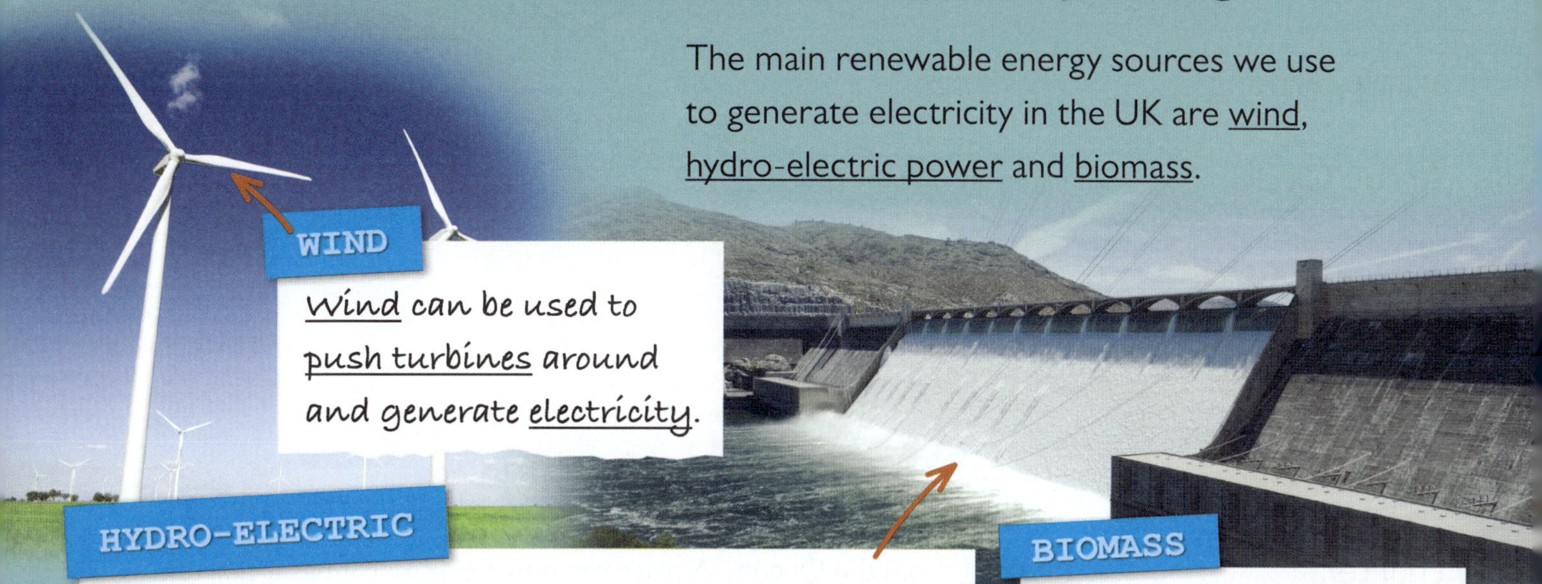

**WIND**

Wind can be used to push turbines around and generate electricity.

**HYDRO-ELECTRIC**

Hydro-electric power means using water that is flowing downhill to turn turbines and generate electricity.

**BIOMASS**

Plants can be burned as a fuel to produce electricity.

Other renewable sources of energy include solar power (from the sun), geothermal (using the heat inside the Earth).

## Diamonds aren't the only valuable rocks

Some countries have lots of valuable minerals (like gold) under their land. They can mine these minerals to use or sell. The UK has a few useful minerals to mine like iron ore and tin.

## Food glorious food

**FOOD**

Food is produced on farms. The UK has arable farms that grow crops and pastoral farms where sheep and cattle are raised. Large areas of land in the UK are used for farming.

**WATER**

Everyone needs water to be able to live and grow food. Most of the water we drink in the UK has to be collected from rain water in huge reservoirs. It is then cleaned and piped into our houses.

*It rains a lot in the UK, so why should we try to save water?*

It's important to try and save water. In the summer months there is often less rain, so UK reservoirs may run low on water. It also costs a lot to clean water and pipe it to our homes.

### It's amazing what you can dig up

Life would be really hard without the food, fuel and minerals we get from the ground.

# Glossary

| | |
|---|---|
| arable farming | Growing crops. |
| Arctic Circle | The area around the North Pole. |
| Antarctic Circle | The area around the South Pole. |
| bog | A wet, muddy bit of land. |
| capital city | The city where the government of a country is based. |
| charter | A document from the Queen. A place can only be a city if it has a charter. |
| chemical plant | A factory that makes chemicals. |
| climate | What the weather is generally like and what it's been like for years. |
| climate zone | The climate in a certain area of the world — the world is split up into six climate zones. |
| condensation | When a gas cools and turns into a liquid. |
| cone (volcano) | The main body of a volcano, which is made up of layers of cooled lava and ash. |
| continent | A large mass of land and the islands closest to it. The Earth has seven continents. |
| contours | Lines on maps that show how high the ground is. |
| crater (volcano) | The hole in the top of a volcano where lava comes out. |
| crust (of Earth) | The thin, solid outer layer of the Earth that we live on. |
| delta (river) | Land formed when water slows down and drops sediment at a river's mouth. |
| deposition | When water 'drops off' the rock, sand and soil it is carrying along. |
| earthquake | When part of the Earth's crust wobbles and shakes. |
| equator | An imaginary line halfway between the poles, running across the Earth. |

| | |
|---|---|
| erosion | When rock is broken down into small bits or worn away by water or the wind. |
| eruption cloud (volcano) | When a volcano releases gas and ash into the air, forming a cloud. |
| estuary | The really wide bit of a river where it joins the sea. |
| evaporation | When a liquid is heated up and turns into a gas. |
| farmstead | A farm, including the farmhouse and the buildings around it. |
| government | A group of people who make the laws in a country. |
| homestead | A house, plus the land attached to it and the buildings around it. |
| infiltration | When water soaks into the ground. |
| inner core (of Earth) | A super-hot solid ball of iron and nickel at the centre of Earth. |
| land use | What people use land for. |
| lava | Magma that comes to the Earth's surface, for example from volcanoes. |
| lines of latitude and longitude | Horizontal and vertical imaginary lines around the Earth. |
| load | All the bits of rock, sand or soil carried along in a river or by the sea. |
| magma | Hot liquid rock underneath the Earth's surface. |
| magma chamber | A pool of magma in the Earth. |
| main vent (volcano) | The main route the lava takes from the magma chamber to the Earth's surface. |
| mantle (of Earth) | The thick, gooey layer of molten rock underneath the Earth's crust. |
| meander | A wiggly bit of a river. |
| mineral | A rock or part of a rock that is often useful to us in some way. |
| mining | Digging up valuable rocks or minerals from underneath the ground. |

| | |
|---|---|
| natural resources | All the things found in nature that we find useful. |
| North Pole | The most northern point of the Earth. |
| outer core (of Earth) | A hot liquid layer of iron and nickel surrounding the Earth's inner core. |
| pastoral farming | Breeding and raising livestock like sheep and cattle. |
| physical geography | Natural features (not made by people) like rivers and mountains. |
| precipitation | Rain, snow or hail that falls to the ground. |
| reservoir | A man-made lake that we get our drinking water from. |
| secondary vent (volcano) | When there is a blockage in the main vent of a volcano, the lava flows through this smaller opening at the side of the volcano. |
| sediment | The rock, sand and soil that is 'dropped off' after being carried along in a river. |
| settlement | A place where people live. |
| source (river) | The start point of a river. |
| South Pole | The most southern point of the Earth. |
| spring | A place where water comes up from underneath the ground to the surface. |
| state (of matter) | A solid, liquid or gas. |
| surface runoff | When water flows over ground to rivers, lakes or the sea. |
| tectonic plates | Pieces of the Earth's crust. |
| transpiration | The loss of water from a plant's leaves. |
| volcano | An opening in the Earth's crust which can let hot magma and ash escape to the surface as a volcanic eruption. |
| water cycle | The cycle of water between the Earth's oceans, sky and land. |
| water vapour | The name for water when it's a gas. |